ALL
ANDALUSIA

HUELVA

CORDOBA

JAEN

SEVILLA

ALMERIA

GRANADA

CADIZ

MALAGA

Editorial Escudo de Oro, S.A.

Aerial view of Seville with two of its most characteristic landmarks: La Maestranza bull-ring and the Torre del Oro.

La Torre del Oro marked the boundary of the Islamic walls and was used to keep watch over movements across the Guadalquivir. Today it houses the city's Naval Museum.

SEVILLE

This is Andalusia, the favourite land for a long time of travellers and tourists from all over the world. On the following pages we shall attempt to show all the splendour, diversity, mysticism and specialness of the region.

Let us begin our trip in Seville, Andalusia's most important city, and one of the most beautiful cities in the world.

The province of Seville is situated in the depression of the river Guadalquivir; it is bounded to the north by the Sierra Morena mountain-range, and to the south by the foothills of the Baetic chains.

Just on the left bank of this old river, known to the Romans as *Betis*, stands old *Hispalis*, the capital of Roman *Baetica*.

Seville enjoys a privileged geography and climate, and the Spanish philosopher and writer Ortega y Gasset said of it that is was "the city of reflections". In addition to these natural characteristics, other attractions are the whitewashed houses, the flower-bedecked balconies, the typical courtyards (half-way between Roman and Oriental ones, but above all Andalusian) and the city's innumerable monuments.

Conquered by Caesar, Seville became the Roman capital of *Baetica*. Captured by the Arabs under the command of Musa in 712, it was called *Ixbilia* and

The imposing structure of the Cathedral with the Giralda graciously emerging from behind.

was destined to become one of the most important cities in Al-Andalus until it was reconquered by Ferdinand III in 1248.

After the discovery of America, colonial trade with that continent found its headquarters in the city, and Seville became the metropolis of the New World.

A whole host of different civilisations have passed through Seville, including Tartessians, Phoenicians, Romans, Vandals, Arabs and Castilians. All of them have left their mark on the city in the shape of monuments decorating it, as well as in the spirit and the undefinable atmosphere which this city has, and which provided inspiration for Velázquez, Murillo, Juan de Mesa, Zurbarán, Bécquer, Mérimée, Rossini and many others.

The pinnacle of Seville's historical importance was the celebration of the 1992 Universal Exposition, conclusively launching the city into the future, harmoniously combining the traditional and the contemporary.

Legend has it that the river Guadalquivir was created especially for Seville but, although this would be difficult to prove, what no-one denies is that in Seville there comes together a series of artistic marvels which without the shadow of a doubt were built for the city's embellishment.

The Golden Tower rises at the foot of the river; it was a defence tower for the city and it is said that its name comes from the fact that it was once covered with gilt mosaics. Its twelve-sided ground-

The chancel, closed off by splendid plateresque railings, is presided over by a huge, magnificent, flowery Gothic altarpiece, a jewel of the art of Christendom.

The vestry contains the monstrance of Juan de Arfe, an exemplary piece of Renaissance work in precious metals.

plan was built in 1220 and the lantern was added in the 18th century.

Together, this tower and the Giralda are Seville's best known monuments.

The Giralda stands on Roman stones, although the building of it dates back to 1184. Between 1558 and 1568 the Cordoba architect Hernán Ruiz crowned it with a body comprising twenty-five bells and an enormous statue of Faith, popularly known as the ''Giraldillo''.

Currently the Giralda complements the majestic cathedral of Seville. Built on the site of Seville's main mosque, the cathedral was consecrated as such in 1248.

The only thing remaining of the old mosque is the Orange-Tree Courtyard, which was once the mosque's *shan*.

The construction of the Cathedral began in 1401, conceived as the second largest in all Christendom. It comprises a Gothic nave and four aisles plus a grand transept which houses the chancel, in turn presided over by one of the most splendid reredoses in Christendom (1482-1525), and is the work of Pieter Dancart and Jorge and Alejo Fernández. The wrought-iron screen enclosing the chancel (1518-1533) was created by Brother Francisco of Salamanca and other artists.

Nufro Sánchez and Dancart worked on the marvellous choirstalls.

The tomb of Christopher Columbus is a work of great

Christopher Columbus' tomb can be found in front of the Gate of San Cristobal or the Prince, a Romantic piece by Arturo Mélida.

majesty, and was created by Arturo Mélida in 1891. The sacristies house priceless treasures, the largest sacristy having the following: the *tenebrario*, a 1559 candelabrum, the Juan de Arfe monstrance (1587), the ivory crucifix of Alonso Cano (17th century), the *Descent from the Cross* by Pedro de Campaña and the Alphonsine tablets (relic from 1280). The sacristy of the chalices holds: the Christ of Mercy, a statue by Martínez Montañés (1604) and paintings by Murillo, Valdés Leal, Zurbarán, Ribera and others. The Chapter and Columbus Libraries have conserved printed documents and manuscripts of great value. The Plateresque Royal Chapel (1550-1575) is in the apse. Inside it there are niches with the tombs of Alfonso X the Wise and his mother. At the foot of the high altar there is a richly-worked silver casket in which lie the remains of King Saint Ferdinand; in the crypt are the tombs of King Peter the Cruel and Doña María de Padilla. Noteworthy amongst the treasures of the Royal Chapel are the liturgical ornaments and the sword of St. Ferdinand.

The cathedral also houses an incalculable number of artistic treasures in the shape of sculptures, paintings, precious metalwork, wrought-iron screens and stained glass windows.

Seville's *Reales Alcázares* is the city's main example of non-religious architecture.

The only thing remaining of its Almohad origins is the Plasterwork Courtyard, with its rectangular ground-plan with arcades and central reservoir.

All people who have passed through this building left their mark in some corner or another. However, the basic Alcázar which can be seen today is that built by King Peter the Cruel, and later reformed by the Catholic Monarchs and Charles V. Noteworthy is the Maidens' Court, which is the most splendid example of Mudejar courts in Spanish architecture.

The most important rooms are the Ambassadors' Hall and the Bedroom of the Moorish Kings. The latter, to the right of the Maidens' Court, possesses the most magnificent doors. Everything in the Am-

bassadors' Hall oozes magnificence: the tilework dado, the doors, the coffering, the dome and so on. On the upper floor the visitor's attention is drawn to the so-called Oratory of the Catholic Monarchs, with a very special altar covered in multi-coloured tiles. A special word should be said about the gardens; the design is a mixture of Arab, Mudejar and Renaissance, being decorated everywhere with fanciful fountains and spouts.

Other non-religious architecture includes the General Archives of the Indies (the Exchange). Designed by Juan de Herrera and dating from the 16th century, the General Archives of the Indies houses the most important documents (maps, letters and files) concerning the discovery and conquest of the Americas. Building on the House of Pilate was begun towards the end of the 15th century and was finished when its owner, the first Marquis of Tarifa, came back from a journey to Jerusalem, hence the mixture of Islamic and Renaissance art in the edifice. Its name derives from the fact that initially the palace was thought to be a reproduction of the Praetorium in Jerusalem. It has a magnificent Renaissance courtyard with an elegant fountain supported by four dolphins. Decorating the corners there are impressive statues depicting Minerva.

In this section dealing with non-religious architecture, special mention should be made of the Town Hall building (a splendid example of Spanish Plateresque), the Baroque Palace of St. Thelmo, and the old Tobacco Factory, which today houses the university of Seville, and which is regarded as being the largest monument in Spain after the Escorial.

As a result of Expo'92, the city has gained a new, well-designed and equipped area: La Isla de la Cartuja, with its large gardens and wide-ranging facilities, particularly leisure facilities.

Cruz de la Cerrajería, in the Plaza de Santa Cruz, original filigree work in wrought iron made in 1692.

El Patio de las Doncellas, in the Reales Alcázeres, displays an exquisite decoration of plasterwork and mocárabes (Reproduction authorised by Patrimonio Nacional).

The April Fair is an important and beautiful fiesta. The decorated stalls, women wearing in their Flamenco dresses and expert horsemen are all essential parts of this festival.

The Plaza de España,
the summit of María
Luisa Park, forms a
200 m diameter
semicircle.

Facade of the Fine Art
Museum, housed in an
ancient Mercedarian
convent.

Main staircase of the Casa de Pilatos. Built in the 16th century, this palace displays rich, Mudejar-style adornment.

A view of the Plaza de América and the Plateresque pavilion, the site of the Archaeology Museum.

Seville also has an important Museum of Fine Arts, housed in an old Mercedarian monastery. Its excellent collection of paintings includes works by Pacheco, Zurbarán, Murillo, Valdés Leal and others. In one of the buildings in the Plaza de América (in the middle of the María Luisa Park) stands the Archaeological Museum, with a great many items of great interest, noteworthy amongst which are *Diana Hunting* and *Mercury*, a bust of Trajan and the Carambolo treasure with its Tartessian origins. When one is in Seville, a walk through its streets,

The Mudejar pavilion, built for the Latin American Exposition in 1929, today houses the Museum of Popular Arts and Customs.

San Telmo Palace stands out because of its spectacular Churrigueresque main front.

quarters and gardens is a must, and if possible preferably in Holy Week or else during the April Fair. We have already mentioned the Alcazar's gardens, but mention should also be made of the Catalina Ribera gardens (just by the walls of the Alcazar), the Murillo gardens and above all those of the María Luisa Park and well as those of Las Delicias (the latter running alongside the banks of the Guadalquivir).

In the María Luisa Park stand the buildings of the Spanish-American Exhibition, together with the Plaza de America and the Plaza de España. Initially these gardens were planned according to a British design, but this was later rejected by Forestier, who re-

designed them with a welter of tilework, ponds and fountains.

It is said that Seville is redolent of orange-blossom, and this can best be experienced in the quarter of Santa Cruz. This quarter may be accessed either via the Alcazar itself, or else from the alley of Santa Marta. It is here that the Jewish quarter was concentrated after the Christian Reconquest. In the 16th century, it was to take the shape it retains today, by a broadening of its fronts, protecting the windows with grilles and lattice-work windows and by building spacious courtyards. In the 19th century, the style of the quarter became consolidated with the plac-

The General Archive of the Indies is located in the Plaza del Triunfo, next to the Cathedral.

ing of iron gates which permitted passers-by a view of the courtyards inside.

In the maze of small backstreets there are those steeped in vitality and legend, as their names suggest: Vida (Life), Agua (Water), Pimienta (Pepper), Gloria (Glory) and Jamerdana. There are also small squares such as that of Doña Elvira, or the one of Santa Cruz in which the wrought-iron cross is found, a highly original work of filigree iron built in the 18th century, and where Murillo lies buried.

From the 16th century, Seville has been celebrating Holy Week with all the fervour that a religious festival of this nature deserves.

The people of Seville are organised into brotherhoods who express their devotion by means of processions of floats on which different scenes of the Passion of Christ are depicted. The statues are usually veritable works of art, by the hand of statue-makers like Martínez Montañés, Juan de Mesa and so on. The brotherhood members, dressed with tunics and conical hoods, accompany the floats which, thanks to the skill of the bearers, move to the rhythm of the trumpets and drums, only stopping when the heart-rending cry of the ''saeta'' (religious song) rings out. All the religious fervour of the people of Seville dresses up in colour for the fiesta of the April Fair.

Easter: the "passing" of Our Lord Jesus of the Passion.

Scene from the Romería del Rocío, a very deep-rooted gathering in Seville. People along the Rocío path to the hermitage of el Rocío in Almonte (Huelva).

Easter: image of Nuestra Señora de la Hiniesta.

Bridge of the Quincentenary, built for the 1992 Universal Exposition, which joins the city to the island of La Cartuja.

One part of the city is given over to the enclosure for the fair, and in it are raised hundred of stands where there is drink and dance to the sound of *Sevillanas*, a typical song and dance.

All along the improvised narrow streets there parade strings of horses decorated with tinkling bells jingle bells, with young women dressed in all their finery. But we should not leave Seville without having tasted its *fried fish* or its *snacks*, to be eaten in any of the many bars or inns, and washed down with the wine from the nearby lands of the province of Cádiz.

Detail of the Alcazar of King Pedro in the village of Carmona.

La Alhambra with the snow-covered Sierra Nevada as a backdrop.

GRANADA

The city of Granada occupies a splendid position. It takes up a broad fertile plain and three hills: Sacromonte, the Albaicín and the Alhambra (separated from the previous two by the waters of the river Darro). And the majestic Sierra Nevada mountain ranges provides a backdrop for the whole city. The origins of the city are associated with the first dwellers, a tribe of Iberians: the Turdules. In the 5th century B.C. the city was mentioned by the name of *Elibyrge* in the Hecateos of Miletos. Already in that period coins were minted, and on them there were allegories to the sun, a practice which was to continue under Roman sway, who built their city *Iliberi* between the quarters of Alcazaba and the Albaicín. Although the Arabs conquered Granada by force of arms, it was thanks to them that the city lived through its period of greatest splendour, especially from 1238 onwards with the founding of a Nasrid emirateship, the magnificence and sumptuosity of which is testified to by the splendid buildings and magnificent gardens which have come down to us today. In 1492 the city was reconquered by the Catholic Monarchs who, like their predecessors, showed special interest in continuing the task of

Garden and Torre de Machuca, where the architect of the Palace of Carlos V lived.

beautifying the capital. The modern city was created, and around the cathedral there arose splendid Renaissance, Baroque and Neoclassic buildings. Noteworthy of all the buildings in the city is, without the shadow of a doubt, the prodigious architectural ensemble of the Alhambra.

This building was raised on the hill known to the Arabs as Asabica (after Alhamar, founder of the Nasrid dynasty) and finished by the successors Yussuf I and Mohammed V, who were responsible for most of the buildings which have survived.

Gate of Justice, dating from the 14th century, opened in a tower in the walls of the Alhambra, and Fountain of Carlos V.

The Mexuar Room, where the council used to meet, turned into a chapel in Christian times.

Located in an old fortress, the Alhambra comprises the Alcazaba (rebuilt by Alhamar) and the Royal House or Palace of the Moorish kings of Granada, where the Arab monarchs had their residence.

The name of the Alhambra comes from the word *calat-alhamra* meaning "red castle", and refers to the reddish colour of the clay in the walls, although the chronicler Aben Aljatib says that this reddish colour is a reference to the fact that the rebuilding of the old fortress was done by night, under the fantastic red glow of the torches.

Mexuar Patio and facade of the Cuarto Dorado.

Detail of the wall of the Patio of the Myrtles. Tiles and calligraphy as decorative elements of an original and unique art.

Gallery of the Patio of the Myrtles which leads into the Sala de la Barca.

The Alhambra has a surprisingly sober exterior, which diguises the treasures to be found within. In order to have access to those treasures, one should pass through the 14th-century Justice Gateway with its large horseshoe arch and carved marble hand on the keystone, a talisman for some against the evil eye and for others the emblem of the five precepts of the Koran: fasting, prayer, alms, pilgrimage to Mecca and belief in the singleness of Allah. The current entry point to the palace leads us to the Mexuar, originally used for the administering of justice and later converted into a Christian chapel. At the back of it there is a small oratory affording a splendid view of the Albaicín.

To the north side of the Mexuar Court there is a three-arch portico preceding the room known as the Golden Room, the work of Mohammed V according to one of the inscriptions. Then one goes on the the great Court of the Myrtle-Trees with its two arcades with seven semicircular arches (the centre one being the largest) supported by richly-worked columns; the other two are longer and more simple. There is a pond in the middle, bordered by myrtle-trees, with marble basins at either end. After the north portico there is the Barca Gallery which precedes the throne room and which must have been used as a waiting room for the royal audiences which were held in the Ambassadors' Hall in the adjacent Comares Tower. This room is the palace's largest, and was the setting for the grand receptions. It is said that in this room it was agreed to surrender Granada to the Catholic Monarchs. It has magnificent stuccowork and tilework on the walls, and excellent cedarwood coffering on the ceiling.

The beautiful Patio of the Myrtles, also called Patio of the Reservoir, the Pool and the Myrtle, was the centre of official activities.

The Ambassadors Room, the largest in the palace, was the setting for major receptions.

The ceiling of the Sala de los Abencerrajes takes the form of mocárabe vaults and a star-shaped dome.

From the Court of the Myrtle-Trees, crossing the Mocárabes Gallery, one enters the well-known Court of Lions, which takes its name from the twelve lions supporting the central fountain. The somewhat rough execution of this ensemble stands in stark contrast to the elegance and delicacy of the surrounding gallery, supported on very slender columns of white marble.

The court communicates with the sumptuous chambers such as the Abencerrajes Gallery, the Kings' Chamber or the Hall of the Two Sisters.

The first of these quarters takes its name from the male members of this family who had their throats cut in this very place, according to legend. Their heads were piled up in the main fountain, and popular tradition has it that the iron oxide stains in the first-class marble basin are in fact those of the Abencerraje blood that was spilled here. The gallery still preserves well-carved and splendidly pure in style capitals painted blue, plus a splendid geometrically-worked dome.

The alcoves of the Kings' Chamber, which might possibly have been royal bedrooms, have ceilings covered with paintings which, judging by their style, are attributed to some Christian artist from the end of the 14th century or the beginning of the 15th. In the central alcove the first ten kings of the Nasrid dynasty appear. In the other alcoves there are hunt-

El Patio de los Leones is surrounded by a gallery supported by 124 delicate columns made from white marble.

The Rest Room, named thus because everything in it is conducive to rest.

Detail of the Rest Room which allows us to appreciate the palace's rich coloured decoration.

ing scenes, tournaments, games and love stories. The Hall of the Two Sisters is covered with a marvellous ceiling of geometric patterns, which because of its perfection is worthy of comparison with the dome of the heavens, according to an inscription running around the wall. A door leads to the Ajimeces Gallery. This room, plus the so-called Daraxa's Belvedere, coming straight after, formed part of the apartments reserved for the Sultana. From Daraxa's Garden one may visit the Grille Court and the Baths.

The restoration of the Royal Baths, carried out in the 19th century, brought back the original golds, blues, reds and greens, and give us an insight of how the palace decoration must have been.

In the east wing of the alcazar are the Partal Gardens, forming terraces until they reach the Ladies' Tower with its graceful portico (partal in Arabic) with its five arches through which access is afforded to a room with a splendid ceiling and to a belvedere which has preserved a major part of its stuccowork. From its windows the river Darro and Sacromonte may be seen.

Now outside the Alhambra, but intimately linked to

Gardens of El Partal and the Torre de las Damas.

Aerial view of the Palace of Carlos V. The circular patio, 30 m in diameter, possesses a double gallery of columns. The bottom ones are Doric and the top ones are Ionic.

The "jarrón de La Alhambra", a masterpiece of Hispano-Arabic ceramics of the 14th century, is one of the major pieces of the Hispano-Muslim Museum which is housed in the Palace of Carlos V.

it, is the Generalife, the summer residence of the Nasrid sovereigns; it is surrounded by luscious gardens with delicately-worked fountains and small spouts.

The 14th-century palace is reached via the Cypress walk and the Adelfas walk. The building comprises two edifices linked to each other by means of the Pond Court, through the centre of which there runs

Patio de la Acequia in Generalife Palace. ▷

"Tríptico de la Pasión", by Dierick Bouts, in the Royal Chapel.

Mausoleum of the Catholic Monarchs in the Royal Chapel, by Doménico Fancelli, in Carrara marble. ▷

The remains of the Catholic Monarchs rest in the crypt of the Royal Chapel.

The crown, the sceptre and the casket of Isabel la Católica and the sword of Don Fernando.

La Cartuja. Cloister.

style, and was built on the orders of the Catholic Monarchs, who wished to be buried in Granada.

The ground plan is in the shape of a Latin cross, and the transept is enclosed by an excellent gilt wrought-iron screen, the work of the master craftsmen Bartolomé de Jaén. Noteworthy are the valuable carvings and Flemish figures, the reredos of the high altar and the tombs of the Catholic Monarchs and their children.

The original Gothic doorway of the chapel, within the cathedral, is decorated with the coats of arms of the Catholic Monarchs.

The cathedral is one of the most outstanding Renaissance churches. Work on it began in 1518 and was finally finished in 1704. The Baroque main front (1667) is a masterpiece by Alonso Cano. Noteworthy inside is the circular and well-proportioned chancel.

In 1506 work was begun on the building of the Charterhouse or Carthusian monastery, located on the Alfacar road. Its sacristy is an outstanding example of Spanish Baroque, a style that was also used in the decoration of the Sancta Sanctorum, and executed by Francisco Hurtado at the beginning of the 17th century.

The Albaicín is also worth a visit. It is an old Moorish quarter which in broad outlines still preserves its original aspect and its old layout. Its streets meander and climb up the hill opposite the Alhambra, bounded by houses reminiscent of the *Moriscos* (Moors converted to Christianity) and the famous *cármenes* or gardens.

From the Plaza de San Nicolás one may enjoy a splendid view of the Alhambra, the Generalife and the lower part of the city.

Half-way up the Cuesta del Chapiz there is a road leading off to Sacromonte which, as it climbs up the mountain, becomes gradually peppered with caves where the gypsy *zambra* is danced, to the sound of clapping and guitars.

The ideal place to acquire a souvenir of the city is, without any doubt, the Alcaicería, which in days gone by was the Arab silk market, and which has been rebuilt to conform to the original layout.

a long channel into which the waters of many fountains flow. It is bounded by with a gallery with arcades and the walls of the residence built in the 16th century.

Before leaving the Alhambra, a visit to the palace of Charles V, built by Pedro Machuca on the Emperor's orders, is a must. Though it offers great contrast with the Arab building, its uncluttered Renaissance style is very worthy of notice. Its great courtyard is thirty metres in diameter, and is one of the most beautiful examples of Spanish Renaissance. The palace houses the Museum of Hispano-Moorish Art.

Of the Christian buildings in the city, the Royal Chapel is noteworthy. It is Flamboyant Gothic in

In front of the Alhambra, houses the stretch up along the hill of the Albacín, on the top of which San Nicolás church is located. It is a magnificent mirador over the city.

The Alcalcería, an ancient Muslim silk market, reconstructed in accordance with original drawings.

Rising high above the city of Granada, the Sierra Nevada mountain range has the highest peaks of the whole of the Iberian Peninsula. Three major summits stand out: Mulhacén (3,482 m), Veleta (3,398 m) and Alcazaba (3,366 m), which stretch southwards down to gentle ridges. A road, considered to be the highest in Europe as it reaches an altitude of 3,390 m, winds its way up to Veleta peak, which can also be reached by cable car. From the heights, there is a splendid panorama: on the Mediterranean side, the view stretches out to La Alpujarra, an area of extraordinary beauty with its countryside of terraced hillsides and changing vegetation, from pine and chestnut trees at the top to the fruit orchards and groves of the valleys; on the Atlantic side, facing towards the city of Granada, the landscape is dominated by sharp profiles with deep precipices and almost vertical escarpments. The Sierra Nevada ski resort is situated at the foot of the Veleta. The resort has a ski area covering some 2,500 hectares. The centre of the resort is called Pradallona and is situated at an altitude of 2,100 m, just 30 minutes from Granada by car. It has all the facilities that any lover of winter sports could ever need, including a High Performance Centre and a wide variety of accommodation and entertainment services. The ski resort, which was founded at the beginning of this century, boasts both national and international recognition. In the summer months, the Sierra Nevada is still very much alive with other sports such as rock-climbing rambling, and horse or mountain bike riding among a whole host of activities in a natural setting whose landscape cannot be bettered.

The Sierra Nevada ski resort lies at the foot of Veleta peak.

Partial view of Malaga, with the bull-ring in the foreground, taken from Gibralfaro hill.

MALAGA

The capital city of Málaga, the "city of paradise" according to the Spanish poet Aleixandre, occupies a privileged place at the mouth of the Guadalmedina, standing oposite the Mediterranean at the foot of Gibralfaro hill.

Its excellent geographical position explains the diversity of people who have passed through it: Phoenicians, Greeks, Carthagininans and Romans to mention a few. Under Arab sway it became the main port of the kingdom of Granada, and was also one of the most important cities in Andalusia. It was reconquered by the Catholic Monarchs in 1487, and has managed to preserve its importance throughout time down to the present. Today is has become a modern city which has flourished thanks to the increase in tourism.

Málaga's rich legacy is a testimony to the wealth of its history, typified above all by the cathedral. This building, constructed to the designs of Diego de Siloé, is a Renaissance building with a Baroque main doorway which was raised on the initiative of the Catholic Monarchs on the spot previously occupied by a mosque.

Work began in 1528 and finished in the 18th century, though the right-hand tower was left unfinished.

Malaga Cathedral was raised between the 16th and 18th centuries. Several master masons worked on it.

Noteworthy inside the cathedral are the chapels of St. Barbara with its splendid Gothic reredos, and the chapel of Our Lady of the Kings which still preseves the (rebuilt) reredos by Pedro de Mena with the praying statues of the Catholic Monarchs done in painted wood. Much of the work on the stalls in the magnificent choir, whose figures are noteworthy for their naturalness and simplicity, is also due to Pedro de Mena.

Other churches of interest are the Shrine church, with its Gothic main doorway and 16th-century high altar reredos from Becerril de Campos in Palencia; St. James church with its exceptional Mudejar tower, and where Picasso was christened; the Baroque churches of St. Peter and St. Dominick; the neo-Gothic church of St. Paul's, and the Sanctuary of the Virgin of Victory, founded by the Catholic Monarchs and rebuilt in Baroque style at the end of the 17th century. Inside this latter church there is a magnificent Madonna, the work of Pedro de Mena, and the impressive 17th-century crypt, the pantheon of the counts of Buenavista. In the church the image of the city's patron saint, the Virgin of Victory, (a 15th-century Gothic carving) is worshipped.

In the calle Alcazabilla stands the main entrance point to the Alcazaba which was built in the 9th century and which was originally the residence of the Arab governors of Málaga. The fortress has three concen-

Patio de la Alcazaba. The Archaeology Museum is housed in this palace, the former residence of the Arab governors, and together with the Gibralfaro Castle, it forms one of the most important monuments of Muslim Malaga.

Gibralfaro Castle, to which access is gained via a zigzag rampart with fortified doors. From the top, the city, mountains and the port are all spread out below.

"El Cenachero", in the Plaza de la Marina, by Jaime F. Pimentel.

Easter: arrival of the student brotherhood. The scene takes place in the Plaza del Obispo, where the Cathedral and the Episcopal Palace are located. The Diocesan Museum is located inside the Palace.

tric walls. Inside there are three courtyards with splendid *Morisco* pools; the Puerta de Granada building houses the city's Archaeological Museum. From the walls there is a magnificent sweeping view of the bay of Málaga.

The Alcazaba communicates with the castle of Gibralfaro via a corridor between the walls. The origins of the castle date back to the times of the Phoenicians, thought the most noteworthy remains are from the days of the Arabs.

The castle has leafy gardens, is surrounded by an attractive landscape, and from its walls one enjoys a magnificent panoramic view of the city, its mountains and the bay.

Image of the Virgen de la Amargura.

The popular Pasaje de Chinitas, a meeting point in the 19th century which today is full of character and holds many memories.

Typical views of Malaga: a caravan of coaches in the August fair, and horse a carriage gracefully adorned.

Torremolinos, just 14 km from Malaga, enjoys long sandy beaches.

Other key places in Málaga are the Plaza de la Merced, where the birthplace of the great genius of painting, Pablo Picasso, stands; another place to be visited is the popular Pasaje de Chinitas.

Close to the cathedral runs the Park Walk, built on land reclaimed from the sea. In its avenues there grow a wide variety of different flowers, subtropical for the most part, and has certain species which are unique in Europe. The Park communicates with the splendid Alameda avenue via one of its ends, leading thence through the Plaza de la Marina where the statues of the Basketmaker and the Jazmine-picker stand.

Two views of Benalmádena: Bil-Bil castle, a modern, Arabic-style building on the shore which houses the Municipal Cultural Centre, and the Promenade and Santa Ana beach.

Fuengirola's fishing
harbour.

San Cristóbal Church in
Mijas, a genuinely
Andalusian-style village.

"Burro-taxi", a charming
aspect of Mijas.

Aerial view of Puerto Banús, a recently built development which has a large harbour.

Far from the city centre, there stands the typical quarter of El Palo, an old fishing village where today one can savour *pescaíto frito* (small fried fish), as well as many other delicious specialities in any of the bustling beach bars.

Málaga has a wealth of traditions and festivities. One of the most popular of them is ''Los Verdiales'', in which songs and dances are performed which are regarded as being even older than Flamenco singing itself.

In Holy Week, the whole of the city of Málaga lives

The old town of Marbella is characterised by its romantic winding streets and white houses.

The New Bridge of Ronda is some 90 m above the cleft of the river Guadalevín.

Vélez-Malaga.

A typical corner of Frigiliana. Aerial of the Torre del Mar. A view of the old town of Estepona. Playa de Calahonda and Balcón de Europa in Nerja.

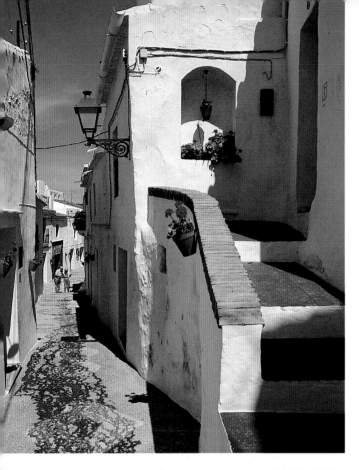

Casares is a picturesque village. There are splendid views from the top of the hill.

A view of the impressive prehistoric caves in Nerja, where the lighting enhances their natural beauty.

through the solemn ceremonies in a flush of emotion: the freeing of a prisoner which is granted by the statue of Jesus ''Nazareno'' each Ash Wednesday; the procession on Maundy Thursday, with the Christ of the Good Death and the Virgin of Bitterness; the procession of the brotherhoods, some of them (like the Students' brotherhood) dating as far back as the 17th century.

The coastlines of the provinces of Granada, Almería and Málaga together form the internationally famous Costa del Sol.

Temperate in climate and short on rainfall, with a great variety of landscapes, the coast of Málaga is dotted with broad beaches, half-hidden coves and villages in which the visitor will find excellent hotel amenities and a wide variety of entertainment and fun.

On the western coastline of the province stands Torremolinos and its long beaches. Almost as a prolongation of this town stands Benalmádena-Costa with its large fun park. Fuengirola runs alongside a very long beach. From here there is a road running to the picturesque village of Mijas. Back on the coastline once more, we now reach the cosmopolitan town of Marbella and its luxurious Puerto Banús. In Estepona the modern marine parade exists alongside the old fishing village centre. Leaving the coast for a moment, one reaches the whitewashed villages of Casares and thence to Ronda, one of the most interesting Andalusian cities. Antequera is an important monument centre, with Renaissance and Baroque works. And once more to the coast, where we will find the broad beach of Torre del Mar and Nerja, a truly privileged spot.

Torre de Calahora, the Roman bridge and, in the foreground, the Albolafía windmill.

CORDOBA

The province of Córdoba is situated in the centre of Andalusia. The river Guadalquivir crosses it from east to west, separating the mountains to the north and the open countryside to the south. Ten centuries ago Córdoba was the capital of Moslem Spain, and in addition to being the largest city in the then known world, it became the greatest cultural and intellectual centre of it too, thus contributing to European civilisation with such great names as Maimonides, Averroes, Aben Hazam and others.

In 1236 the city was conquered by Ferdinand III, the Saint King. It was also the sometime court of the Catholic Monarchs, and it was here that Isabella determined to lend her support to the adventure proposed by Columbus.

Today Córdoba is a city filled with monuments, a city in which art is to be found in every corner such as alleys, courtyards, squares and so on.

Córdoba, amongst other things, is known for its mosque. Nonetheless, also worthy of mention are the old Arab and Jewish quarters, as well as its noble mansions.

The art of the caliphs in the West finds its high-water mark in the Moslem mosque which dates back to the 8th century, and which was consecrated as a Christian cathedral in 1236. Two worlds, two cultures are

Two views of the Mosque: a forest of columns, and the west and south facades.

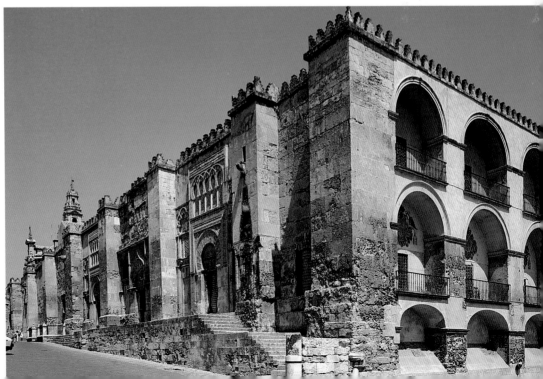

Door of the Mosque, caliphal decoration.

The bell-tower and the old minaret of the Mosque-Cathedral.

exquisitely combined in it. The Moslem mosque was finished at the end of the 10th century, when Al Mansur was the prime minister of Caliph Hisham II. It was built over a Visigothic cathedral. The mosque comprises a fascinating maze of columns with red-and-white and green bands.

One of the most important features of the mosque is its *mihrab*, where faithful Moslems said their prayers. It is an octagonal-shaped room topped by a marvellous dome, delicate work on the arcading and priceless mosaic work, the whole thing a gift from Emperor Constantine VII to the Caliph Al Hakam II. In the Moslem mosque there is also a concentration of art works of great value by the hands of masters such as Valdés Leal, Pedro de Córdoba, Alsonso Cano and so on.

Right in the centre of the mosque stands the Christian cathedral, work on which was begun in 1523 during the reign of Charles V, although it was finally finished in 1776 when the choir and the pulpits were terminated. There is a mixture of architectural styles in it: Renaissance with reminiscences of Gothic, Plateresque, Herrerian and Baroque. The high altar reredos should be singled out for special mention. It is built in red marble and is decorated with paintings by Palomino. The Churrigueresque pulpits were built by the French sculptor Michel de Verdiguier, as was the choir.

Entrance to the mihrab, a room decorated with extraordinary sumptuosity.

Dome of the maxura of the mihrab, of perfect geometrical progression and exquisite beauty. A present from emperor Constantine to caliph Alhakem II.

The super-imposed, multi-lobed arches of columns of red and blue marble that precede the mihrab.

Eighteenth century choir-stalls, by Pedro Duque de Cornejo, made from Indies mahogany, with scenes from the Old and the New Testaments, of the life of the Virgin Mary and Cordovan martyrs.

Central aisle of Cordoba Cathedral. The high altar is presided over by an altarpiece containing marbles by Carcabuey, canvases by Antonio de Palomino and gold-leaved wooden sculptures by Pedro de Paz.

Monuments to three illustrious Cordovans: Maimónides (1135-1205), doctor and thinker of Hebrew origin, in La Calle de Judíos; the philosopher Averroes (1126-1198), whose statue is raised next to the walls; and the Aben Hazam (994-1064), next to the Gate of Seville.

Gardens of the Alcazar of the Christian Kings, where water is of primordial importance, as a mark of the Arab tradition.

Around the mosque there is a whole series of Christian chapels: the chapel of Our Lady of the Conception, of St. Peter, of St. Lawrence as well as others. Leaving through the Pardon Doorway we come to the Orange Tree Courtyard. Via the Deans' Doorway we find the St. Jacintus Doorway and then the Bishop's Palace, where the Visigoth governors once resided.

One of the best examples of 14th-century military architecture is the Alcazar (fortress) of the Christian Kings, built in 1328 on the orders of Alfonso XI. It

The Plaza del Potro is one of the most representative corners of Cordoba.

comprises three towers: the Lions' Tower, that of the Alliance and the River Tower. Inside there is a large collection of mosaics and a richly-worked Roman sarcophagus.

In the Jewish quarter we find the 14th-century synagogue with important stucco-work.

Córdoba also has a magnificent series of churches, which merge together differing styles, as well as important museums which display the best examples of different artists and Córdoba's folk traditions.

El Cristo de los Faroles is the object of most deep-rooted popular tradition.

Exuberant vegetation and whitewashed walls are a characteristic feature of the Cordovan patios, which are at their best during the Cordovan Patio Contest held during the May festivals.

Monument to Monalete, an illustrious native of the city, and the Church of Santa Marina de Aguas Santas.

"Poema a Córdoba" by Julio Romero de Torres, in the house-museum of this great Cordovan painter.

The Cordovan people fervently celebrate Easter making their "steps" in a solemn procession.

Two views of the ruins of Medina Azahara. Built in the 10th and 11th centuries by the first caliph Abderramán III, this magnificent palace-city became the symbol of caliphal splendour.

ENVIRONS OF CORDOBA

The environs of Cordoba, the countryside to the south and the mountains to the north, give the visitor the chance to make enjoyable excursions to enjoy different types of scenery. The Sierra also contains a number of sites of outstanding interest: At the foot of the so-called Monte de la Desposada are the ruins of the palace city of Madinat al-Zahra, or **Medina Azahara**. Construction began in 936 under Abderramán III, first Caliph of Al-Andalus, apparently in honour of his favourite, Al Zahra, but, in 1010, was completely sacked and burnt down in the course of the Fitna, or civil war. In 1910, archaeological excavations began here, an arduous task of reconstruction thanks to which we can now visit some of the rooms and marvel at the decorative wealth of this fabulous site, once a symbol of the splendour of the caliphs.

Near to Medina Azahara is the **Monastery of San Jerónimo de Valparaíso,** founded in the early 15th-century. It is now owned by the Marquis of Mérito. Conserved of the original building are the chapterhouse, the prior's cell and the Gothic cloister, a two-storey construction of austere beauty. The church was reformed during the baroque period.

In the Sierra, on the mountain known by some as La Cárcel and by others as La Víbora, are the **hermitages of Córdoba**. The present hermitages were built between 1703 and 1709, though they date back originally to the time of the Moorish occupation. They currently pertain to the Carmelite Order, and stand in a site presided over by the spectacular monument to the Sacred Heart of Jesus, by Coullant Valera in 1929.

Aerial view of Jaen Cathedral, whose monumental dimensions overwhelm the old city.

JAEN

Jaen is situated in the centre of Andalusia, between Cordoba and Granada, at the foot of the Jabalcuz mountain range.

The city was called *Geen* (road or way for caravans) by the Arabs, and traditionally, the place has been called the ''Gateway to Castile''.

Jaen still preserves a very interesting old part with a very clear Arab influence.

The city's most important monument is its cathedral, built on the spot once occupied by an older mosque. In it there are to be found Gothic, Plateresque, Renaissance and Baroque elements.

Building began in 1550, the master architect being Andrés de Vandelvira, who was succeeded by his pupil Alonso Barba. The main front and the vaults were not completed until the Baroque period.

The main front is flanked by twin towers, decorated with bas-reliefs and sculptures by Pedro Roldán. The front opens as a balustrade with statues of St. Ferdinand, the great doctors of the Church and the Evangelists.

The interior is designed in the shape of a Latin cross. The nave and two aisles end in vaults supported on stout Corinthian columns.

In the middle of the nave stands the choir with its magnificent back wall and 15th and 16th-century

Main facade of the Cathedral, by Andrés de Vendelvira, also architect of the sacristy.

Two views inside the Cathedral: the grandiose nature of the setting and choir display great ornamental richness.

choirstalls. The chancel preserves the relic of the Holy Face, thought to be one of the sheets used by Veronica to wipe the face of Christ; it is contained within a reliquary made of precious stones.

The cathedral museum is housed in the crypt of the sacristy. The cathedral boasts valuable examples of art, among them items by master Bartolomé, Alonso Cano, Martínez Montañés and so on.

Abutting the cathedral is the Shrine church, built in the 18th century by Ventura Rodríguez.

Other interesting churches are St. Mary Magdelene's, St. Andrew's (Mudejar with Jewish reminiscences which make it look like a synagogue), the chapel of Mary the Most Pure (abutting the previous building,

Easter: "passing" of Jesus of Nazareth.

and which has a painting on board depicting the Virgin of Populo, plus a gilt wrought-iron screen, a masterpiece by master Bartolomé). There is also the convent of the Discalced Carmelites, where the original manuscript of St. John of the Cross's *Spiritual Chants* may be admired; the church of St. Ildefonsus with its Gothic, Renaissance and Baroque fronts; the monastery of St. Clair, one of the oldest in Jaen and where there is till conserved a highly-appreciated bamboo carving of Christ, possibly from the Quito school, and the College of St. Dominick, which was once a convent and an Arab palace, a dwelling place for St. Ferdinand and headquarters of the Holy Inquisition. Its front boasts an excellent piece of work by Vandelvira as well as a splendid cloister with Tuscan columns.

Special mention should be made of the Provincial Museum. Here may be seen the doorway of the church of St. Michael by Vandelvira, Porcuna's "Iberian Bull" and some others valuable items.

In the city there are also interesting examples of non-religious architecture which witness the historical importance of Jaen. Losing oneself in its narrow cobbled alleys, we shall discover numerous mansions and palaces which contrast admirably with the whitewashed houses with their purple roofs. Thus we have the palaces of the Vilches, the Vélez, the Uribe and the Mudejar remains of the palace of the

Constable. Dominating everything is the castle of St. Catherine, which had now been converted into a Parador (state-run luxury hotel), which was built by King Alhamar and rebuilt by Ferdinand III. This castle affords a splendid panoramic view stretching from the Sierra Morena mountain range to the Sierra Nevada.

Part of the walls descending from the castle, which once surrounded the old city, are still standing. The solid towers in the Calle del Obispo, the tower in the house of Count Torralba, and the archway of St. Lawrence are all good examples.

Ubeda and Baeza are both some 50 km from Jaen, both towns being veritable showcases of art and history.

In monuments in Baeza one may run the whole gamut of architectural styles, ranging from Mudejar to Gothic and Baroque. Thus we have the Romanesque church of St. Cruz, the Romanesque church of the Saviour with its Mudejar interior, and the Renaissance church of St. Andrew.

Baeza has an admirable collection of public buildings: the original Gothic Town Hall, the old University, the old prison, the old slaughterhouse, the corn exchange, and Gothic palaces such as those of Jabalquinto and Montemar.

Ubeda lies very close to Baeza. This town has been called "the Salamanca of Andalusia" thanks to the quality of its monuments, such as the Renaissance Holy Chapel of the Saviour, and the Gothic-Mudejar

A wide panorama stretching from the Sierra Morena to the Sierra Nevada is appreciable from the Santa Catalina Castle (12th century).

A view of the city of Baeza with the arches that were built in Carlos V's honour: The Gate of Jaen and the Arch of Villalar.

church of St. Mary of the Royal Alcázares amongst others.

There is above all an endless list of Renaissance palaces such as those of Dean Ortega, Constable Dávalos, that of the Marquis of Mancera, of La Ramba, and the Hospital of St. James, (mid 16th century), the most noteworthy non-religious building in the town.

This notwithstanding, we should not bid farewell to the province of Jaen without a stroll around the narrow alleyways of the inner city quarters of Ubeda.

Baeza: Plaza de los Leones.

Ubeda: The 16th century Holy Chapel of the Saviour, designed by Diego de Siloé and built by Andrés de Vendelvira, is one of the major works of the Renaissance.

The city of Cazoría, with the tower of the Castle of La Yedra in the foreground.

The imposing pile of the Alcazaba presides over the city of Almería.

ALMERIA

Standing at the back of the bay bearing the same name, the city of Almería is a light-filled city, sheltered from the inland winds by its ochre-coloured mountains which reflect the intense blue which the waters of the Mediterranean take on here.

The city's origins date back to prehistory. Later it was the point of contact with East Mediterranean cultures and later still visited by the Carthaginians, Romans and Arabs, who called it "Mirror of the Sea".

Reconquered by the Catholic Monarchs in 1484, the city conserves the testimonies of its historical impor-tance. One of these, the Alcazaba, dominates the city with its massive bulk.

The fortress must have been built by Abd ar-Rahman III in the 10th century, with a capacity for more than 20,000 men. It is irregular in shape and is distributed into three staggered enclosures. The keep has two 15th-century Gothic doorways with the coats of arms of the Catholic Monarchs.

From the parapet walk there is an excellent panoramic view of the city and its port.

The old walls (of which some sections still stand) runs around the city via the La Joya ravine and St. Christopher's Hill, where some fortified towers

The Alcazaba, with the picturesque houses of the Chanca quarter around it.

The choir-stalls of Almería Cathedral were made by Juan de Orea in a plateresque style.

Tomb of Friar Diego Fernández de Villalán, in one of the side chapels, the bishop who encouraged the construction of the church.

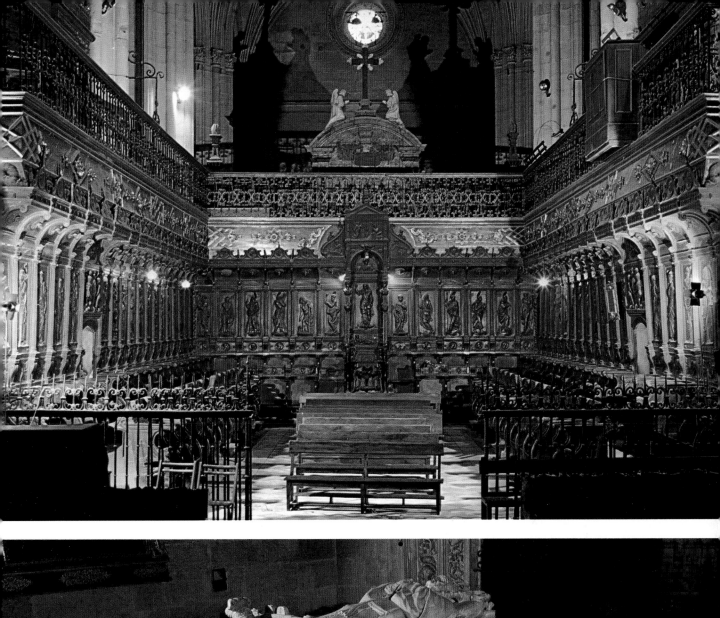

Nicolás Salmerón Park, next to the port.

belonging to the castle of the same name still stand. At the feet of the Alcazaba lies La Chanca, the popular fishermen's quarter where the houses, many of them simply caves cut into the hillside, have fronts made of alternating whites and the most eye-catching colours.

Almería's cathedral causes some surprise since it has all the appearance of a fortress. It was built in the 16th century, and its defensive architecture was designed as a protection against pirate attacks which the city suffered from constantly during those times. In spite of its outward severeness, it has two door-ways of great decorative elegance.

The spacious interior is divided into a Gothic nave and aisles with side chapels; one of them houses the magnificent tomb of the bishop who was a prime mover in the building of the cathedral, Fernández de Villalán; others hold valuable works by Salzillo, Alonso Cano, Murillo and Ribera. Also noteworthy are the high altar and the pulpits, the Plateresque choirstalls and the 18th-century retrochoir, decorated with alabaster statues.

Almería is a city that lives for and from the sea. Proof of this is provided by its port, where fishing boats alternate with large ships which transport the bumper harvests of flowers and fruit produced in Almería. Near the port area, the Breakwater Gardens are worth a visit, as are the quarters of St. Peter's Wharf, and the square in the Puerta de Purchena, the Plaza Vieja or the Plaza de la Virgen del Mar and so on. The capital also possesses interesting outskirts with beaches like those of Aguadulce or Roquetas del Mar.

The province of Almería is full of contrasts, ranging from the fertility of the countryside around Dalias to the desert landscape in the neighourhood of Tabernas, where more than one Wild West film has been made. Tabernas still preserves the remains of a castle where Isabella the Catholic spent the night during the siege of Almería.

The ''hanging houses'' of Sorbas are perched atop

City Hall building, in the Plaza de la Constitución, where the Monument to the Martyrs of Freedom "Los Coloraos" was raised.

Almería's fishing harbour.

a rocky outcrop, cut off by a deep ravine which acts as a sort of natural fosse.

Níjar conserves its very original crafts: its ceramics with their Phoenician origins, and its fabrics (called *jarapas*, manufactured from strips of different material.

Mojácar is a very special and splendid nucleus, with its white houses nestling together around a hilltop. Carboneras is a fishing village situated on a broad beach. In Vélez Blanco stands the castle and stately home of the Vélez family; in Laujar, a place steeped in history, the river Andarax is born in the midst of a beautiful landscape.

The western road is cut out from high cliffs. The San Telmo Castle serves as a beacon.

Arco beach on the Isleta del Moro.

Cape Gata dunes.

Mojácar, on the foothills of the Sierra Alhamilla.

Ragcloth is a one of the original crafts still preserved in Nijar.

View of Vélez-Blanco with the stately castle of the Marquis of Vélez.

Cadiz Cathedral.

CADIZ

Cádiz, the "little silver cup", is a magnificently situated sea-faring city, and is one of the most attractive capital cities of Andalusia.

With its three thousand years of history, the Phoenician *Gadir* is the oldest settlement in the Iberian peninsula, and possibly the most ancient of the whole western world.

Within its 18th-century walls (some sections still standing), the city cherishes rich monuments, of which the cathedral, regarded as being the capital's most important monument, is the most noteworthy. The building is Neoclassic. Work on it was begun by Acero in the 18th century and was not finally concluded until the 19th century.

The cathedral museum has a splendid collection of precious craft work, the most noteworthy item (amongst others) being the "Million" monstrance, so-called because of the enormous number of precious stones used in the making of it.

Cádiz is embellished by a large number of walks, beaches and gardens. In the Plaza de la Constitución there stands the Earth Gateway (Puerta de Tierra), one of the five let into the walls. In the well-known Plaza de San Juan de Dios stands the Town Hall, a Neoclassical building; in the Plaza de España stands the Cádiz Parliament building, and finally the city looks out over the ocean through the Apodaca and Marqués de Comillas avenues, the latter more accurately being a magnificent garden which stretches as far as the Genoa Park.

Deeply steeped in its sea-faring tradition, Cádiz retains a good deal of fishing activity. It has a large

The city has a
magnificent location,
joined to the mainland by
a narrow, sandy isthmus.

Avenida Ramón de
Carranza.

The Gate of Earth, flanked by the two patron saints of Cadiz, San Servando and San Germán.

trading port, and to the south of the bay may be made out the whiteness of the San Fernando salt pans. In February Cádiz celebrates its famous carnival, an event that has been declared of Tourist Interest. All towns and villages in Cádiz are worth a visit. Ranging from those up in the mountains, with their white houses, down to the coast, not forgetting the towns and villages in the fertile route of the wine. Jerez de la Frontera owes its name to its world-famous wines, which may be tasted in the local wine-cellars. It also has a wealth of monuments with splendid mansion houses and churches such as St.

Plaza del Tío de la Tiza.

Cadiz Cathedral, baroque style with neoclassical elements, was built between 1720 and 1838 in accordance with Vicente Acero's plans.

In the Plaza de España, a monument to the Cortes de Cádiz was raised.

James', St. Matthew's, St. Mark's, the Collegiate church, and so on. The astounding village of Vejar, perched on a limestone outcrop, still retains its Arab layout, where buildings such as the parish church, built over an older mosque, are most noteworthy. Algeciras occupies a strategic location on the bay of the same name, lying only 25 kilometres from the North African coast. It is a cosmopolitan city with intense tourist traffic, and also has important monuments such as the church of La Palma, as well as important archaeological remains. La Línea de la Concepción is a modern town which stands at one end of the bay of Algeciras and borders with Gibraltar.

Carnival in Cadiz has been listed as being of International Tourist Interest.

Vejer de la Frontera, listed as National Heritage, rises up on top of a hill cut off by a stream. At the top, the ancient Arabic castle and the Church of the Divine Saviour stand out.

La Línea de la Concepción and, in the background, the Rock of Gibraltar.

Various aspects of wine producing. Along the "wine route" of Cadiz, besides Jeréz de la Frontera, there are Trabujena, Sanlúcar de Barrameda, Chipiona, Rota and El Puerto.

Cathedral of La Merced.

HUELVA

Huelva is the westernmost province of Andalusia. Its coastline (called the Costa de la Luz, or Light Coast) stretches from the mouth of the river Guadiana at the Portuguese border, to the Tarifa on the Straits of Gibraltar.

Currently it is one of the favourite haunts of tourists thanks to its enormous stretches of sand, pine groves and the typical features of its fishing villages such as Ayamonte, Isla Cristina, Lepe, Matalascañas or Punta Umbría.

The mountain villages and towns are equally worthy of mention: Aracena, Cortegana, Jabugo are just some of the names filled with colour and flavour.

Huelva, the capital marvellously situated at the confluence of the rivers Tinto and Odiel, stands in the middle of the province.

The city of Huelva stands on the shores of the sea, and offers us its streets, backwaters and squares... squares like the quiet Plaza de San Pedro where the church of the same name stands, as well as a monument to Archpriest Don Manuel González García, and where the old Town Council met; then there is the Plaza de las Monjas, one of the most welcoming meeting places in Huelva.

In 1755 Huelva suffered a terrible earthquake which almost completely razed it to the ground; however, three very interesting churches survived: the church of Mercy, that of the Conception and St. Peter's.

El Muelle Gardens.

The first of these churches is also a cathedral and was built in the 18th century. It possesses a statue of the Christ of Jerusalem (12th century) and a splendid image of the Virgin of the Ribbon, by Montañés. Huelva's most popular church is that of the Conception, built in the 16th century and rebuilt after the earthquake.

St. Peter's church is the oldest of the three and was built on the site of an older mosque, still conserving traces of Mudejar.

Huelva has always distinguished itself for its seafaring activities, but without any doubt it was the discovery of America that really put it on the map of history.

City Hall.

The Church of San Pedro (16th century), in the square of the same name, is the oldest in Huelva. Raised over the remains of an ancient Arabic mosque, it conserves Mudejar-style traits. The bell-tower was added in the year 1772.

Prawns are one of the major gastronomic specialities of the area.

Today the city's port facilities are the scene of intensive activity both in mining and fishing products. Just on the edge of the port area, there runs the Palmeras walk, a sort of oasis of calm in the midst of so much hustle and bustle in and around the port. In the estuary of the river Tinto stands Palos de la Frontera, the exact geographical point from which Columbus set forth on his search for the Indies. At

At La Punta del Cebo, the confluence of the Tinto and the Odiel, the Monument to Colombus was raised.

Palos de la Frontera, the port of departure for Colombus on his way to the Indies.

The Monastery of La Rábida was built in the 15th century in a Gothic-Mudejar style.

the confluence of the Tinto and the Odiel, at the Punta del Cebo, there stands the monument to Columbus. This great white statue was sculpted by Gertrudis Whitman and was a gift from America to Spain.

The route followed by Columbus on his voyages must necessarily include the names of Moguer, Palos and the monastery of Santa María de la Rábida.

The first three sailors to enlist on the caravelles came from Moguer; the great Spanish poet Juan Ramón Jiménez also comes from the same place. Palos is "the land of all enterprise in the discovery of the Americas" by definition. And it was through the St. George gateway (also called the "fiancés gateway")

that Columbus and the Pinzones set forth on the 3rd August 1492.

On the eve of his departure Columbus had prayed all night in the convent of La Rábida for the success of his venture.

The convent is simple in construction but nonetheless very interesting; it has a Gothic main front, a light-filled cloister, important frescoes by Vázquez Díaz and a small Gothic-Mudejar church.

On Whit Sunday thousands of pilgrims or *romeros* from Huelva, Cádiz and Seville wend their way to the Shrine of the Virgin "del Rocío" in Almonte, to render homage to the "White Dove". The event has a long tradition and enjoys immense popularity.

Hermitage of El Rocío, in Almonte.

Room of fresco paintings by Daniel Vázquez Díaz, relating to the discovery of America, in the Monastery of La Rábida.

The popular Romería del Rocío.
Coto de Doñana, nature reserve.
Gibraleón, with the river Odiel in the foreground.

General view of Aroche.
The Castle of Almonaster la Real.
The saltpans of Isla Cristina.
Ayamonte leisure port.

Contents

Collection ALL EUROPE

	Spanish	French	English	German	Italian	Catalan	Dutch	Swedish	Portuguese	Japanese	Finnish
1 ANDORRA	●	●	●	●	●	●					
2 LISBON	●	●	●	●	●				●		
3 LONDON	●	●	●	●	●					●	
4 BRUGES	●	●	●	●	●		●				
5 PARIS	●	●	●	●	●					●	
6 MONACO	●	●	●	●	●						
7 VIENNA	●	●	●	●	●						
11 VERDUN	●	●	●	●				●			
12 THE TOWER OF LONDON	●	●	●								
13 ANTWERP	●	●	●	●	●		●				
14 WESTMINSTER ABBEY	●	●	●	●	●						
15 THE SPANISH RIDING SCHOOL IN VIENNA	●	●	●	●	●						
16 FATIMA	●	●	●	●	●				●		
17 WINDSOR CASTLE	●	●	●	●	●					●	
19 COTE D'AZUR	●	●	●	●	●						
22 BRUSSELS	●	●	●	●	●		●				
23 SCHÖNBRUNN PALACE	●	●	●	●	●		●				
24 ROUTE OF PORT WINE	●	●	●	●	●				●		
26 HOFBURG PALACE	●	●	●	●	●						
27 ALSACE	●	●	●	●	●		●				
31 MALTA		●	●	●	●						
32 PERPIGNAN	●										
33 STRASBOURG	●	●	●	●	●						
34 MADEIRA + PORTO SANTO		●	●						●		
35 CERDAGNE - CAPCIR		●				●					
36 BERLIN	●	●	●	●	●						

Collection ART IN SPAIN

	Spanish	French	English	German	Italian	Catalan	Dutch	Swedish	Portuguese	Japanese	Finnish
1 PALAU DE LA MUSICA CATALANA	●		●			●					
2 GAUDI	●	●	●	●	●					●	
3 PRADO MUSEUM I (Spanish Painting)	●	●	●	●						●	
4 PRADO MUSEUM II (Foreign Painting)	●	●	●	●						●	
5 MONASTERY OF GUADALUPE	●										
6 THE CASTLE OF XAVIER	●	●	●	●						●	
7 THE FINE ARTS MUSEUM OF SEVILLE	●	●	●	●	●						
8 SPANISH CASTLES	●	●	●	●							
9 THE CATHEDRALS OF SPAIN	●	●	●	●							
10 THE CATHEDRAL OF GIRONA	●	●	●	●		●					
11 GRAN TEATRO DEL LICEO	●	●	●								
11 EL LICEO ARDE DE NUEVO	●					●					
12 THE CATHEDRAL OF CORDOBA	●	●	●	●	●						
13 THE CATHEDRAL OF SEVILLE	●	●	●	●	●						
14 PICASSO	●	●	●	●	●					●	
15 REALES ALCAZARES (ROYAL PALACE OF SEVILLE)	●	●	●	●	●						
16 MADRID'S ROYAL PALACE	●	●	●	●	●						
17 ROYAL MONASTERY OF EL ESCORIAL	●	●	●	●	●						
18 THE WINES OF CATALONIA	●										
19 THE ALHAMBRA AND THE GENERALIFE	●	●	●	●	●						
20 GRANADA AND THE ALHAMBRA	●										
21 ROYAL ESTATE OF ARANJUEZ	●	●	●	●	●						
22 ROYAL ESTATE OF EL PARDO	●	●	●	●	●						
23 ROYAL HOUSES	●	●	●	●	●						
24 ROYAL PALACE OF SAN ILDEFONSO	●	●	●	●	●						
25 HOLLY CROSS OF THE VALLE DE LOS CAIDOS	●	●	●	●	●						
26 OUR LADY OF THE PILLAR OF SARAGOSSA	●	●	●	●	●						
27 TEMPLE DE LA SAGRADA FAMILIA	●	●	●	●	●	●					
28 POBLET ABTEI	●	●	●	●		●					
29 MAJORCA CATHEDRAL	●	●	●	●	●	●					

Collection ALL SPAIN

	Spanish	French	English	German	Italian	Catalan	Dutch	Swedish	Portuguese	Japanese	Finnish
1 ALL MADRID	●	●	●	●	●					●	
2 ALL BARCELONA	●	●	●	●	●	●				●	
3 ALL SEVILLE	●	●	●	●	●					●	
4 ALL MAJORCA	●	●	●	●	●						
5 ALL THE COSTA BRAVA	●	●	●	●	●	●					
6 ALL MALAGA and the Costa del Sol	●	●	●	●	●						
7 ALL THE CANARY ISLANDS (Gran Canaria)	●	●	●	●	●		●	●			
8 ALL CORDOBA	●	●	●	●	●					●	
9 ALL GRANADA	●	●	●	●	●					●	
10 ALL VALENCIA	●	●	●	●	●					●	
11 ALL TOLEDO	●	●	●	●	●						
12 ALL SANTIAGO	●	●	●	●	●						
13 ALL IBIZA and Formentera	●	●	●	●	●						
14 ALL CADIZ and the Costa de la Luz	●	●	●	●							
15 ALL MONTSERRAT	●	●	●	●	●						
16 ALL SANTANDER and Cantabria	●	●	●	●							
17 ALL THE CANARY ISLANDS II (Tenerife)	●	●	●	●	●		●	●			●
20 ALL BURGOS	●	●	●	●	●						
21 ALL ALICANTE and the Costa Blanca	●	●	●	●	●		●				
22 ALL NAVARRA	●	●	●	●							
23 ALL LERIDA	●	●	●	●		●					
24 ALL SEGOVIA	●	●	●	●	●						
25 ALL SARAGOSSA	●	●	●	●	●						
26 ALL SALAMANCA	●	●	●	●	●				●		
27 ALL AVILA	●	●	●	●	●						
28 ALL MINORCA	●	●	●	●	●						
29 ALL SAN SEBASTIAN and Guipúzcoa	●										
30 ALL ASTURIAS	●	●	●								
31 ALL LA CORUNNA and the Rías Altas	●	●	●	●	●						
32 ALL TARRAGONA	●	●	●	●	●						
33 ALL MURCIA	●	●	●	●							
34 ALL VALLADOLID	●	●	●	●							
35 ALL GIRONA	●	●	●	●							
36 ALL HUESCA	●	●	●	●							
37 ALL JAEN	●	●	●	●							
40 ALL CUENCA	●	●	●	●							
41 ALL LEON	●	●	●	●							
42 ALL PONTEVEDRA, VIGO and the Rías Bajas	●	●	●	●							
43 ALL RONDA	●	●	●	●	●						
44 ALL SORIA	●	●									
46 ALL EXTREMADURA	●	●	●	●							
47 ALL ANDALUSIA	●	●	●	●	●						
52 ALL MORELLA	●	●	●	●		●					

Collection ALL AMERICA

	Spanish	French	English	German	Italian	Catalan	Dutch	Swedish	Portuguese	Japanese	Finnish
1 PUERTO RICO	●		●								
2 SANTO DOMINGO	●		●								
3 QUEBEC			●	●							
4 COSTA RICA	●		●								
5 CARACAS	●		●								

Collection ALL AFRICA

	Spanish	French	English	German	Italian	Catalan	Dutch	Swedish	Portuguese	Japanese	Finnish
1 MOROCCO	●	●	●	●	●						
2 THE SOUTH OF MOROCCO	●	●	●	●							
3 TUNISIA	●	●	●	●							
4 RWANDA		●									

PORTUGAL

CIUDAD REAL

ALBACETE

BADAJOZ

MURCIA

○ Belacazar
○ Hinojosa de Duque
Fuenteovejuna ○ Pozoblanco
Peñarroya-Pueblonuevo
Río
Río Guadiato
○ La Carolina
○ Villacarrillo
Andújar Bailén
Linares
Cazalla de la Tierra
○ Constantina
Posadas
CORDOBA
Montoro
Baeza Ubeda
○ Rosal de la Frontera
Jabugo
Aracena
Santa Olalla
Lora del Río
Ecija
Martos
JAEN
Cazorla
Vélez Blanco
Valverde del camino
Baena
Huescar
Baza
La Palma del Condado
SEVILLA
Alcalá de Guadaira
Carmona
Montilla
Cabra
Aguilar de la Frontera
Alcalá la Real
Huércal-Overa
HUELVA
Marchena
Osuna
Lucena
Loja
Priego de Córdoba
A-49
Utrera
A-92
Guadix
GRANADA
Vera
Cuevas de Almanzo
Ayamonte
Moguer
Almonte
Coria
Morón de la Frontera
Antequera
SIERRA NEVADA
Garrucha
Mojácar
Isla Cristina
Punta Umbría
Palos de la Frontera
Olvera
Orjiva
Sorbas
Tabernas
Carboneras
COSTA DE LA LUZ
PARQUE DOÑANA
Ronda
Vélez-Málaga
Almuñecar
Berja
ALMERIA
Sanlúcar de Barrameda
Jerez de la Frontera
Arcos de la Frontera
Coin
Nerja
Motril
Albuñol
Roquetas
Cabo de Gata
Chipiona
El Puerto de Sta María
SERRANIA DE RONDA
MALAGA
Torremolinos
Fuengirola
COSTA DE ALMERIA
CADIZ
San Fernando
Chiclana de la frontera
Vejer de la Frontera
San Roque
Marbella
S. P. de Alcántara
Estepona
COSTA DEL SOL
MAR MEDITERRANEO
La Línea
Gibraltar
Algeciras
ESTRECHO DE
Tarifa
GIBRALTAR
Ceuta
Tanger

ESCALA GRAFICA
0 10 20 30 40 50 km.